I believe it is written
in your destiny
that you will survive
life's challenges
triumphantly.

Other Books by Donna Fargo
Published by
Blue Mountain Arts®

Ten Golden Rules for
Living in This Crazy,
Mixed-Up World

To the Love of My Life:
A Collection of Love Poems

Trust in Yourself:
Thoughts About Listening to Your
Heart and Becoming the Person
You Want to Be

I Prayed for You Today

A Collection of Uplifting Thoughts to Let Someone Special Know How Much You Care

Donna Fargo

Blue Mountain Press™

Boulder, Colorado

Scripture quotations on page 31, except where noted, are from The Holy Bible: New International Version. Copyright © 1973, 1978, 1984 by The International Bible Society. All rights reserved. Scripture quotation marked NKJV is from New King James Version Bible. Copyright © 1982 by Thomas Nelson, Inc. All rights reserved.

Library of Congress Control Number: 2005900853
ISBN: 978-0-88396-923-6

Certain trademarks are used under license.
BLUE MOUNTAIN PRESS is registered in U.S. Patent and Trademark Office.

Printed in the United States of America.
Second Printing: 2007

 This book is printed on recycled paper.

This book is printed on fine quality, laid embossed, 80 lb. paper. This paper has been specially produced to be acid free (neutral pH) and contains no groundwood or unbleached pulp. It conforms with the requirements of the American National Standards Institute, Inc., so as to ensure that this book will last and be enjoyed by future generations.

Blue Mountain Arts, Inc.

P.O. Box 4549, Boulder, Colorado 80306

Contents

I Prayed for You Today

I prayed for you today, gave thanks for your life, wished you the best, asked the heavens to bless you with good health and happiness. I sent you good thoughts, surrounded you with hope and faith and love. I asked your guardian angels to protect you and keep you safe from any harm and to blanket you with joy and contentment and peace and prosperity.

I prayed for you today. I asked that you be guided with the wisdom to make choices to enhance your life and the awareness to make changes that are in your best interest. I wished for you a storehouse of opportunities, the ability to meet your goals, and the joy of your own approval and acceptance. I wished for you your heart's desire, every need met, every prayer answered, and every dream come true.

I prayed for you today. I asked that you be prepared for whatever life hands you or whatever you're going through. I asked that your spirit be strong and lead you and guide you each step of the way down every path you take. I asked the universe to confirm for you that you're someone very special. I asked the Earth to be good to you, and I asked God to show you His perfect way. I prayed for you today.

I Know You Can Get Through Whatever Life Hands You

*E*ven when things may not seem to be working out the best for you, I know you, and I know that you'll make the best of any situation.

I know that you will keep on doing everything you can — a day at a time. It will take courage, discipline, and perseverance to get to where you want to be, but I know you'll get there.

Try not to worry. Try to look at what you're going through as a time to make full use of your abilities. Have faith in God, have confidence in yourself, and believe that you're going to be fine.

Take authority over your troubles. Don't let them cause you to give up. Learn from them. Feel them lose their power over you. Allow them to teach you what you want to know, and then move on.

You're a survivor. You're going to handle whatever comes along. You're going to find strength you didn't know you had and grace to deal with whatever you need to. Pretty soon, you'll be on the other side and you will look back on this time in your life when you replaced your fears with faith and determination and were rewarded with answers to your prayers.

I'll Be There for You in Every Way That I Can Be

*W*hen there are clouds in your sky...
If there's something you want to bounce off
someone, I'll listen.
If you want to cry, I'll do what I can
to help you dry your tears.
When you need to be alone, I'll give you
your space, but I'll walk with you through
the storms if you want me to.
If you're down, I'll encourage you and we'll
chase hope and laughter till we catch them.

And when there's sunshine in your life...
If you want someone to celebrate with,
I'll be happy for you.
If you need to brag a bit on yourself,
that's okay, too.
When you're on cloud nine, I'll be there with
you to soak up the sun and share your joy.
If you want someone just to have fun and
enjoy the day with, I'm ready.

Between the sunshine and the clouds
during the highs, the lows, and
all the in-betweens,
I just want you to know that I'll be there for you
in every way that I can be.

Here's What I'd Do for You, If I Could...

I'd help you reach your goals and supply your every need. I'd put magic in every day for you. I'd heal every hurt you've ever known and help you solve every problem you have. I'd pay your bills and dissolve your debts, help you live your life with no regrets... I would. I really would.

I can't do all that, but I can wish and hope and pray for you. I can try and plan and help you to find a way. I can dream and scheme, and I can think of you. And I can believe and have faith and never give up for you.

I know it's easy to say you'd do something for someone if you could, but if it's the thought that really counts, then I'm thinking of you. And if I could help you find the key to every door you want to open, I hope it matters to you that... I would. I really would.

...Because I Really Care About You

I think you already know this, but in case you need reminding, I'll say it again... You are so special to me. You are loved. You are appreciated. You are an inspiration, a blessing, and an important person in my life.

And because I care about you, I have so many wishes for you... I wish you love. I wish that you could spread your wings and fly to that special place in your heart and mind where you would have everything you want and need, without a care or worry in the world. And then I wish that your desires could be so real that you would feel the sun shining just for you, hear the birds singing special songs for you, smell the flowers blooming just for you, and know that everyone who matters to you cares for you, too.

Hang In There

Life's full of surprises — some good and some not so good. When your world has been turned upside down, it probably feels as though there's confusion every way you turn.

But just remember... there are clearer skies and brighter days after a hard rain, and this stormy weather in your life will also change. Life hurts sometimes, but that hurt will eventually become a memory with valuable lessons learned.

When you're going through a difficult time, try to go with the flow, do the best you can, be patient, and believe that the sun will shine again. Life has its seasons, but seasons change.

Trust that all things will work out eventually for the good. Search your heart with clear vision to make the best decisions for your life and to find healing light to get you through every dark place. Believe that things will get better. It's just a matter of time. Hang in there.

Let's Believe...

*L*et's believe that...
  Doors that are closed can also open.
  Where there's a will, there's also a way.
  We have the answers inside us to every
    question we have.
  Determination gets results, persistence counts,
    and our attitude matters.
  We can make a difference, positive or
    negative, in our lives and in our world.

Let's be assured that...
  There's power in faith, and all things are possible.
  Thinking and hoping are more important
    when they give birth to action.
  We are rewarded for our efforts and our faith.
  God is on our side, not against us.
  Our life is a gift to us, but we must take
    responsibility for its quality.

Let's trust that...
  The problems we face are challenges in life,
    not punishments from God.
  We can choose peace, no matter what we're experiencing.
  Motivation and sacrifice often work together
    to help us move forward.
  Desire and awareness create the way for positive change.
  When our words and actions are in sync,
    there's no stopping us.

In Times of Doubt, Say These Words to Yourself...

Bring on the sun. I'm tired of the rain.
Give me some heat. I don't like the cold.
I need some light. I'm sick of the darkness.
On with the new stuff and out with the old.

Where is my hope? I can't go on without it.
I need to be up. I don't want to be down.
I want my blessing. I'm tired of the struggle.
Give me my smile. Take away this frown.

It's time for a change, and I'm gonna make it.
Nothing can stop me. I'll do what I need.
If you don't believe me, you just watch me.
It's gonna happen. I'm planting my seed.

And it's gonna grow. I just know it.
It's time to get going and stop standing still.
This mountain will move, and I'm gonna make it.
I'm on my way. I can and I will.

When Life Puts a Mountain in Your Way, Don't Forget...

You've faced mountains before.
Don't be afraid. You're strong.
Stare it in its face.
Imagine yourself reaching your goal.

Your attitude can free you
or keep you bound.
You have what it takes.
You have your spirit, mind, and body
and the wisdom to know how to compensate.

Cry if you want. That's okay.
Kick and scream. That's okay, too.
And after you get all that out of your system,
put your worries in your suitcase
and check them at the gate so you can
lighten the load and start climbing.

Remember... it's just another mountain.
You've climbed mountains before,
and you will climb this one.
You can do it. Absolutely!

10 Big Things to Remember During the Ups and Downs of Life

1. Your life is a gift to you. Appreciate this gift with all your heart.

2. Know that God is with you wherever you are and no matter how you feel. Pray to Him often, listen to His guidance, and don't forget to thank Him for your blessings.

3. Respect your body. It's the only one you have. Make wise choices about what you feed it.

4. A balanced life is based on give and take. Give joyfully out of your own need, and you will draw whatever you need to you.

5. The choices you make will work for or against you. Your thoughts, words, and actions paint the total picture of who you are. Be as good as your word, and be good.

6. Treat others as you would want to be treated, no matter how they've treated you. A clear conscience and a pure heart are essential for your own integrity.

7. Don't judge others; it's not good for you. Don't try to change others; it won't work. You'll have enough trouble changing yourself.

8. When you're down, get up and try again. Know that whatever you're going through will look different on another day.

9. If you wrong someone, ask forgiveness, and when someone wrongs you, be quick to forgive. Don't forget to forgive yourself, too.

10. Love is the basis of life and the center of all things good. Choose to love others, for when you show love, you are keeping God's greatest commandment and making a positive difference.

Follow the Light, and Look for the Rainbow

I hope you'll find ways to make the difficult times easier, your cares lighter, and the days brighter. I pray that revelations and secrets will unfold for you to make a difference in your life now.

I hope you'll tap into that source of strength that I know is within you, that place where hope and courage live and new dreams are born. I hope you will connect with the kind of faith that helps you to reach your desired goal. I hope you'll gain wisdom and knowledge from this experience, as you find ways to deal with the changes you're having to make in your life.

I believe there's a rainbow after every storm, a light at the end of every tunnel, and hope after every disappointment and struggle. I'm thinking of you and believing that you will find solutions to every problem and answers to every question you have. I believe that prayers can make a difference, and I just know your rainbow will be coming up soon.

See Yourself Doing Better

Examine the pictures you replay in your mind. If your thoughts and actions are contributing to your realities, answer for yourself whether or not you need to change your thinking and the pictures you're developing. It's so important to stay focused on what you want, not on what you don't want.

Sometimes our thoughts re-enter our minds like a steady rain, and depending on the nature of the thoughts, we may be encouraging or discouraging ourselves. If you're recycling pictures of what you don't want, replace those pictures with images that you do want. Put as much emotion into your desires as possible, and visualize your dream in as much detail as you can to create the potential to make it real.

When you notice old fears and doubts showing up without your invitation, change the pictures, just as you would take new snapshots with a camera. Your conscious effort will be a message to your body that you're honoring yourself. Your body will appreciate the attention and reward you. You will feel that you have more power and more confidence to make the changes you need to make.

Don't Let Anything Steal Your Joy

*C*hoose to be well in every way. Choose to be happy no matter what. Decide that each day will be good just because you're alive. Don't let your circumstances dictate to you how to feel. Don't let your thoughts and feelings color your situation blue or desperate. You have power over your thoughts and feelings. Use this power.

Even if you don't have everything you want, even if you're in pain or in need, even if you're having health or financial issues — whatever is bothering you — you can choose to be joyful. You are more than your body, your physical presence, and your material possessions. You are spirit. You are God's child, and you are blessed.

When you're able to change something that needs changing, you will. Decide that life is good and you are special. Decide to enjoy today. Decide that you will deal with whatever you need to deal with in the way that is right for you and in your own time. Decide that you will live life to the fullest now, no matter what, with whatever circumstances you're experiencing. Decide that you're not going to put off living life to the fullest just because things aren't perfect.

Decide that you will not settle for less when you could have more. Don't think you're not good enough to have whatever you desire. Don't think that you don't deserve the best; think that you do because you do. Don't worry about not being perfect; don't worry about some mistakes you've made. If you've asked for forgiveness and been truly sorry, you must accept your forgiveness instead of recycling your regrets by reminding yourself of them constantly. You must break the negative bonds that hold you captive, and you will. It starts with a decision. It begins when you initiate positive thoughts into your thinking. Stop holding things against yourself. Start where you are. Do the best you can. Accept yourself as enough. Decide to steadfastly refuse to let anything steal your joy.

You're the One Who Is Writing Your Story

Life is a wonderful mystery that we must solve. Just as our dreams choose our hearts to live in and our lives to bless, sometimes fate presents us with certain events that we didn't choose but nevertheless must deal with. How we respond to our circumstances makes our stories uniquely our own.

This is where you come in. You're the perfect dreamer of your dreams, and in every chapter of your life, you are the hero who will figure out how you will shape your destiny. Determine to make wise choices, and resolve to take responsibility for your future.

There are beautiful surprises and gifts of wonder waiting for you. Believe the best for yourself. Trust that your body, mind, and spirit are cooperating with you to help you find constructive solutions to your problems. Listen and respond accordingly as you embrace your extraordinary life.

Keep on believing. Your story is a masterpiece unfolding.

The Choice Is Yours

*I*n the quiet of your heart and mind, there may be times when you'll be afraid, but don't be.

Fear creates negative scenarios in our minds. It invites along all its friends: worry, blame, guilt, loneliness, depression, and doubt. Each time we allow ourselves to dwell in fear, it stirs the dark side of the imagination and can make things seem worse than they are, adding one more "what if?" after another. It can steal our joy, add harmful stress, and take our focus away from positive possibilities.

Have a healthy respect for fear, but don't give it more attention than it deserves. Let it make you cautious; let it help you to protect yourself. Don't let it cause you to get bogged down to the point that you lose your courage and hope. Use fear to give you the power to keep yourself optimistic and to give yourself confidence that you've done all you can.

None of us can know exactly what the future holds, but we can choose our attitude toward what we're facing. Fear can be helpful or hurtful. You can choose how you deal with it and how it will affect you.

Don't Give Up

Your wings may be a little damaged now, but you can still fly. You can still touch the sky. You're hurt, but you can still dream. You can still try. You might have to do things a little differently, but you can do them.

As you dodge these curve balls that are coming at you now, don't let anyone take away your hope, get you down, or make you give up. While you face these problems that touch the land mines in your soul, don't let them steal your power. Stay strong, encouraged, and hopeful.

Refresh your spirit with the lessons you've learned. This is just a passage you're going through. You know your heart. You know who you are. There will be answers. Be satisfied with doing the best you can. When you're down, don't stay there.

Life Is Good and It's on Your Side...

Sometimes our opinions may need slight adjustments for us to get what we want. We may need to consciously decide to let go of old feelings that bind us and hold us back in order to allow the impossible to become possible. Sometimes we're our own worst enemy, and the answers we are seeking are very simple.

The mind is probably the hardest thing to change; it doesn't react too well to force or sometimes even to knowledge. But just being willing to change an attitude that has existed for a long time can allow change to happen and solutions to come. Sometimes we have to get out of our own way to find our way; we have to shift from feelings of doubt to simple, childlike trust.

We can't always select our experiences; there will be surprises that we didn't plan. But we can choose how we perceive a situation — as a problem or an opportunity. We can find a way to use our own innate gifts and come up with approaches that are best for us. The answers we're seeking may be only one action away, and all it takes is admitting we need help and saying "I am willing to change my way of thinking."

...and God Is on Your Side, Too

I am the Lord your God, who teaches you what is best for you, who directs you in the way you should go. *(Is. 48:17)* ➔ Who takes hold of your right hand and says to you, Do not fear; I will help you. *(Is. 41:13)* ➔ I have loved you with an everlasting love; I have drawn you with loving-kindness. I will build you up again. *(Jer. 31:3-4)* ➔ I am concerned for you and will look on you with favor. *(Ez. 36:9)* ➔ Do not be afraid; do not be discouraged. *(Deut. 31:8)* ➔ I will not forget you! *(Is. 49:15)* ➔ With everlasting kindness I will have compassion on you. *(Is. 54:8)* ➔ Call to me and I will answer you and tell you great and unsearchable things you do not know. *(Jer. 33:3)* ➔ Do not throw away your confidence; it will be richly rewarded. *(Heb. 10:35)* ➔ Whatever you ask for in prayer, believe that you have received it, and it will be yours. *(Mark 11:24)* ➔ He who overcomes shall inherit all things, and I will be his God and he shall be My son. *(Rev. 21:7, NKJV)* ➔ For nothing is impossible with God. *(Luke 1:37)*

You Are Not Alone

He's with you in the morning
He's with you in the night
He sees through every tear-stained glass
    window of your soul
He loves you just the way you are
    even when you feel you are nothing
He knows the question and the answer
    and the way to reach your goal

He's with you in the good times
    when everything is perfect
He's with you in the bad times
    when you have lost your way
He knows the fears that confound you
    and keep you from receiving
He sees the faith in all your efforts
    and hears every prayer you pray

He's in the thoughts that tiptoe barefoot
    along the banks of your heart
He's the landlord of your soul and
    your mind
He won't impose His will on you, but
    He'll help you make your own choices
When you struggle for the answers that
    you want so much to find

He made the wonders of the universe
    the sun and moon and stars
The rain clouds and the water in the
    cool country stream
He's in your father and your mother
    and every good-luck, four-leaf clover
He lives in your heart and knows every
    dream you dream

When you think you're alone in this place
    called life, don't be afraid
God is with you all the time

You Will Get Your Smile Back

When you're feeling off balance or puzzled by the detours life puts in your way, trust that things will eventually get easier. Your hurts will melt into lessons learned. There will be peace and possibilities, and you will feel better again.

The twinkle will come back to your eyes. There will be a skip in your step and a big sun in your sky. The melody will play again to the song in your heart. Eventually hope will replace discouragement. There will be answers to your questions and resolutions to your conflicts.

Your smile will come back and things will get better. Just remember... those who care for you are standing with you, praying for you, and believing that there will be a favorable outcome for all you're going through.

I Believe in You

When you're very fragile or tough as nails
When you're slow to understand or
    quick to jump
When you want to talk or you want
    to listen
I hope you know that I'm on your side
    and I believe in you

When you play by the book
    or break some of the rules
When you've gone too far or not far enough
When your heart is broken or it's on the mend
I hope you know I'm thinking about you
    and I believe in you

When you're counting your losses
    or flaunting your wins
When you're short on courage
    or you have too much pride
When you're having a hard time
    believing in yourself
I hope you know that I'll be with you
    wherever you are and I believe in you

When your hope is high
    or your confidence is low
When you're trying too hard
    or not hard enough
When you're on top of the world
    or down in the dumps
I hope you know that I'm on your side
    and I believe in you

Take Things One Step at a Time...

*I*n this fast-paced world, we often fall into the trap of wanting everything now, this instant. We want the "quick fix" or no fix at all; unfortunately, the solutions to life's problems don't always come in instant packages. That kind of thinking, when applied to goals that require a series of actions, will keep us from accomplishing our objectives.

To get from the bottom step of a ladder to the top one, you have to take it one step at a time. That's just the way life is — one thing after another — and the results are cumulative.

It's easy to procrastinate, but don't put off starting something you need to do just because you can't see the results of your efforts immediately. Come up with a plan. Go to work, put tomorrow on the back burner, and start to accomplish what you want to do today.

...and Always Be Thankful

When we're in one of those valleys in life, the last thing we probably want to hear from someone is to count our blessings. But if we stop to think about those who are less fortunate than we are, we can almost always think of something to be thankful for. Our shoes may hurt right now, but at least we can be grateful that we don't have to walk in theirs.

Trials may scare us, soften us, mold us, and make us humble, but they will also show us strengths we didn't know we had. Even as we fuss and fight with ourselves over how to get through what we have to go through, in the end we will find that we love a little deeper and appreciate being loved a little more because of what has happened to us.

Although this deepened awareness may not alter what we're going through, getting more in touch with the hidden places in our souls helps us feel a little better and shows us that a thankful heart is truly blessed.

May You Find Answers to the Prayers That You Pray

May you find the gold at
    the end of your rainbow
May you chase every dark
    cloud away
May you find a way to
    open doors of opportunity
May you find answers to the
    prayers that you pray

Looking back, you see only what
    was fact, what was true
Looking ahead, you see your future
    and you dream of a way
As you gather up all your wishes
    and hide them in your heart
May you find answers to the prayers
    that you pray

May you find a bridge to your calling,
    a life raft to save you
May the roadblocks move out of
    your way
For every doubt that confounds you
    and every fear you encounter
May you find answers to the prayers
    that you pray

If you keep trying to reach it
    but your goal is elusive
If you don't know whether to
    move on or to stay
I wish you starships to guide you
    and angels to hold you
May you find answers to the
    prayers that you pray

Someone Cares for You, and That Someone Is Me!

*I*f you're wishing you had someone who hopes that life is being good to you, that you're coping well with every challenge and reaching the goals you want to reach...

If you're feeling alienated from the world, with no one on your side, and you're questioning if there's another human being who would even be concerned about what's going on in your life...

If you're hoping that there is someone in your corner of the world that you could call on any time, someone with whom you could share your hopes and dreams and disappointments...

If you need someone to talk to, to share your worries with, to wish for you perfect health, prosperity, and peace and happiness...

If you want someone to point out your good qualities because you just need lifting up, someone who would be there no matter what and who would go with you whatever distance you have to go...

> Then look no further than my direction, and don't give it a second thought. Know that someone is thinking of you and someone cares about you, and that someone is me.

Caring Thoughts from Me to You

For that dream you wish to come true,
    I hope it does.
For some problem you want solved,
    I hope you solve it.
For a health issue you're trying to change,
    I hope you find a way.
For more prosperity in your life,
    may you receive it.

For satisfaction for a job well done,
    may you find it.
For recognition that you need, I hope it comes.
For relief from some worry, may you find peace.
For the faith that your wishes are truly possible,
    may you believe.

If you want to go someplace you've never been,
    I hope you can.
If there's a change you need to make to be
    happier, I pray you will.
If you need a miracle, I hope your prayer will
    be answered.
If it's a phone call from someone you'd like to
    hear from, may you get it.

If it's a visit with someone you'd like to see,
    I hope it happens.
If there's some material thing you'd like to have,
    I hope you get it.
If you need forgiveness so you can move on,
    may that come to pass soon.
If you need more love in your life,
    may your heart be filled to overflowing.

For Those Times That You Are Discouraged...

There will be times that you'll feel down. There may be days when you'll think that things will never change and you're going to feel this way forever. But for every sunset, there's another sunrise, and for every problem, there's a way to solve it.

This place you're in now is just a place; you will get beyond it. Believe that with all your heart. Rest and trust. Refuse to entertain doubt. Choose to be optimistic. Don't be afraid to regroup and try again if you fail.

Most important, don't allow yourself to give up. You may be discouraged now, but you will get over this. You're strong and creative. You're good and you're loving. You're industrious and you're deserving. You'll be fine. I just know it.

Believe!

There is no one like you. You may have certain limitations, but you also have unlimited potential. You can do anything you believe you can and be anything you can imagine. Look inside your heart with renewed hope and know that your prayers will be answered.

Believe that there's a field of positive energy surrounding you, like a power source, just waiting for you to engage it. Go into this field. Embrace it. Give it a chance to empower you, to love you back. Interact with it. Let the light in and let it light you up. It will prepare you for anything you have to face in life.

Allow your mind and spirit to take you wherever you want to go. See yourself with your very own prize, your most coveted accomplishment. Say out loud what you want. Ask for it. Realize that speaking your desire from your heart is like planting a seed, and saying "Thank you" is the water that makes it grow.

Be Gentle with Yourself

Be good to yourself. Stay strong. Keep the soil of your heart nourished with faith in your hopes and your dreams. Listen to what you're saying to yourself. Is it what you believe, or are you using language that just recycles your fears? Are you talking yourself out of blessings or calling them to be? Are you being as good to yourself as you are to others? You encourage them. Don't forget to be gentle with yourself, too.

Ask God for what you want. Then trust that He heard you and will answer your prayer. Don't be anxious about it. Just relax. You're doing the best you can and that's enough.

Believe that the laws of the universe are impartial and fair to everyone, including you. Don't accept any discouraging thoughts that you hear yourself repeat. Remember that your heart hears everything you say. It's listening in.

Learn from your mistakes and go on. Get in touch with your own intuition and become friends with it. This voice is your very own spirit talking to you, looking out for you and trying to help you. Don't ignore it. Practice listening and being sensitive to its guidance. Tell yourself the truth, but don't punish yourself with regrets and feelings of blame. What's over is over. If you've asked forgiveness, trust that you're forgiven... because you are.

Focus on the Good Things

Make every day a day to celebrate life. With thankfulness, look to every day as a day of new beginnings, opening your heart to absolute hope and unlimited potential.

Take time to pull yourself away from all the noise and just look around you. Appreciate those who have enhanced the quality of your life, and remember that they have been a gift to you. Also remember that you're a gift to them, too.

Look at the choices you've made, both good and bad. Accept your mistakes; you can't change them anyway. Apply what you've learned and go on. Use these lessons to help you with your other decisions in life.

Embrace the universe. Enjoy the colors of the landscape. Soak in the atmosphere. Smile at the world. Don't allow any self-defeating attitudes to creep into your consciousness. Feel the power of your own acceptance. Put a hopeful spin on every thought you have.

Make every day special. Own it. Enjoy it. Bask in the glory of life.

My Hopes for You Are Many

I hope you will look at all your good qualities and realize how important you are to those who love you. Reflect on your own attitude, your accomplishments, and all the things that make you who you are.

Pray for others; especially forgive those who have wronged you. Forgiveness is the grace by which we show personal growth and make progress in our character. It lightens our burdens and sets us free.

As you ease from one day to another, I hope you find time to contemplate the miracle of your own life and the beauty of your own humanity. Enjoy the present. Be optimistic about your future. Allow yourself to dream, and believe that your dreams can come true. Realize the potential in every promise and every hope.

I pray that a band of ministering angels will hover around you and protect you and shield you from harm. I pray that God will be with you wherever you are and keep you safe and sound.

I wish you peace and satisfaction and the continued ability to stand against any resistance you face. May you win your races and pass your tests. May the seeds of faith that you've planted produce a harvest soon!

May no fear touch your doorstep. May no doubts cloud the windows of your soul. May every impossibility be turned into a working blueprint that will help you overcome any challenge that lies before you. May you carry on with love in your heart, wings for your flight, and endless possibilities to reach your goals.

You Can Always Talk to Me

We share the everyday stuff of life. We help each other to put things in perspective when life surprises us with a challenge or someone tries to hurt us, and we can talk about something big or nothing much at all. We provide each other with another point of view, particularly when things aren't going so great. No matter what the situation is, you're never too busy to care about what I'm going through, and I hope you know that I'm always here for you.

I'm Just a Phone Call Away

*I*f there is anything I can do to help make things easier for you, let me know. It's hard when life adds another curve in a road with enough curves already, but I know you are strong and you'll be fine.

I'll tell you what I'm sure you'd tell me in a situation like this: you have good judgment, so just keep on doing your best. You're smart and you always make wise decisions. Be sure to get your rest, and if you want to talk, gripe, cry, laugh, whatever... I'm as near as the phone.

10 Rules for Surviving in This Crazy World

1. Your life is <u>your</u> life. Take responsibility for it. Protect it; cherish it; appreciate it; enjoy it. Above all, don't waste it.

2. Pray a lot. Ask God for guidance and forgiveness when you need it. It will help you move the roadblocks that keep you stuck.

3. With every important action you're considering, think about how you'll feel afterward. Settle important issues before you get taken by surprise and do something that you'll be sorry for later.

4. Never try to persuade others to do something they're not comfortable with, and don't allow yourself to be coerced against your own will either. We each have our own needs and voices; something could be right for one and not right for another.

5. Always be who <u>you</u> are. Learn from others, but be careful to find your own truth.

6. No matter how people act toward you or what they say about you, always do the right thing. You'll never regret it.

7. When you don't know what to do for someone in need who is reaching out, pray and believe that God will allow them to discover whatever will help.

8. Remember that preventing a problem is always easier than fixing one, especially when it comes to your health.

9. Always listen to your heart, trust what you hear, and do what you believe is right for you. Don't waste a lot of time just talking.

10. At all times, find something to be thankful for.

Keep on Listening to Your Heart

You've had more than your share of hurts and adjustments to make. I'm sure that at times it has seemed as though life's good fortunes have eluded you and sweet breaths of relief have been few and far apart. Yet you've demonstrated so much strength and held steady when the tests were difficult.

I just want to encourage you to keep on listening to your heart and being who you are. I rejoice with you at every sign of hope, every moment of renewal. I'm so thankful for you, and I celebrate the person you are.

I Wish You Blessings...
Big and Small

I wish you little things, like...
    a warm fire in your heart when the
      world seems cold
    the feeling you get from falling snow or
      a walk on the beach
    confidence when you're uneasy and your
      self-esteem is low
    opportunities when you think they're out
      of reach

I wish you little things, like...
    a kind word when you are afraid and you
      need direction
    a friendly smile and helpful hand when life
      is tough
    the sound of music and laughter to put
      your troubles in perspective
    signs of hope when you don't have enough

I wish you big things, too, like...
joy with all its resplendent glow and
a fulfilled life
every one of your needs met and all
your dreams come true
someone to hold you close and tell
you that you are loved
lasting friendships with special people
who really care for you

And I wish you even more big things, like...
perfect health in your body and satisfaction
in your soul
peaceful sleep, good memories, and
personal success
unconditional acceptance and forgiveness
when you need it most
closeness with God, prosperity,
and happiness

You Are a Treasure to Me and You Are Always in My Prayers

A treasure is something really special... something irreplaceable, something you wouldn't want to lose for anything... something you value highly, hold close to your heart, protect and appreciate so much. The special people in our lives are treasures to us, and I want you to know what a treasure you are to me.

I can't think of anyone who could take your place. My world is so much better with you in it. Because of your presence in my life, I am more steady and balanced, more confident and secure. I appreciate you more than I know how to say.

You are such a rare and beautiful person, and I will always believe in you. I wish you answered prayers, fulfilled dreams, and the very best life has to offer. Nothing will ever change how much I care about you. Even though words seem inadequate, I want you to know that you are a treasure to me and you are always in my prayers.

About the Author

With her first album, *The Happiest Girl in the Whole U.S.A.*, which achieved platinum album status and earned her a Grammy, Donna Fargo established herself as an award-winning singer, songwriter, and performer. Her credits include seven Academy of Country Music Association awards, five Billboard awards, fifteen Broadcast Music Incorporated (BMI) writing awards, and two National Association of Recording Merchandisers awards for bestselling artist. She has also been honored by the Country Music Association, the National Academy of Recording Arts and Sciences, and the Music Operators of America, and she was the first inductee into the North America Country Music Association's International Hall of Fame. As a writer, her most coveted awards, in addition to the Robert J. Burton Award that she won for "Most Performed Song of the Year," are her Million-Airs Awards, presented to writers of songs that achieve the blockbuster status of 1,000,000 or more performances.

Prior to achieving superstardom and becoming one of the most prolific songwriters in Nashville, Donna was a high school English teacher. It is her love of the English language and her desire to communicate sincere and honest emotions that compelled Donna to try her hand at writing something other than song lyrics. *I Prayed for You Today* is Donna's third book of poetry and follows her other bestselling titles, *Trust in Yourself* and *To the Love of My Life*. Her writings also appear on Blue Mountain Arts greeting cards, calendars, and other gift items.